Presented To

Presented By

Date

Peace I leave with you; my peace I give you.

I do not give to you as the world gives.

Do not let your hearts be troubled

and do not be afraid.

JOHN 14:27

BLESSINGS

—for the—

MORNING

Prayerful Encouragement to Begin Your Day

SUSIE LARSON

BETHANY HOUSE PUBLISHERS
a division of Baker Publishing Group
Minneapolis, Minnesota

Published by Bethany House Publishers
11400 Hampshire Avenue South
Bloomington, Minnesota 55438
www.bethanyhouse.com

Bethany House Publishers is a division of
Baker Publishing Group, Grand Rapids, Michigan

Printed in China

Library of Congress Cataloging-in-Publication Data
Larson, Susie.
    Blessings for the morning : prayerful encouragement to begin your day / Susie Larson.
       pages cm
    Summary: "Reminders of God's promises, love, and purpose for readers to start their days filled with uplifting encouragement and biblical truth"—Provided by publisher.
    ISBN 978-0-7642-1293-2 (cloth : alk. paper) 1. Bible—Devotional literature. I. Title.
BS491.5.L37 2014
242'.8—dc23   2014012201

Cover design by Brand Navigation

Interior design and art direction by Paul Higdon

All images © Shutterstock Photography

Author is represented by The Steve Laube Agency

15   16   17   18   19   20   21   10   9   8   7   6   5   4

To Lizzie and Kristen
God loves you deeply
And so do we

To Jesus
May You breathe fresh life into every soul
who picks up this book.
Knowing that we get to spend eternity
with You is the greatest blessing of all.
You're our greatest treasure.

Contents

To You, My Friend

God loves you with an everlasting love. He is faithful, wise, and true. He is a miracle-working, soul-saving, life-transforming God. And He cares deeply about you.

As you work your way through these pages, may you grow to know—on a much deeper level—what you possess when you have Christ. He is above all, in all, and through all. He is the way, the truth, and the life. He promises never to leave you, never to forsake you, and never to let go of your hand. Life on earth is hard sometimes, but life with God is always good, always beautiful, and forever eternal. The Lord wants you to last long and finish strong, and He's the one who will keep you strong to the end.

May these blessings be yours in every way.

—*Susie Larson*

Also, please don't miss the blessings near the end of the book for specific needs and occasions, including a Restful Weekend, Stepping Out in Faith, No Condemnation, Christmas Eve, Christmas, and the End of Year.

Blessings for the Morning

Have I not commanded you?

Be strong and courageous.

Do not be afraid; do not be discouraged,

for the Lord your God will be with you

wherever you go.

JOSHUA 1:9

Persevere With Feisty Faith

May you make up your mind to persevere and not quit.

May you refuse to be bullied by your fears or diminished by your insecurities.

May you rise up in the knowledge that God made a masterpiece when He made you!

May you embrace the grace to abound in every good work in spite of enemy opposition.

Overwhelming victory belongs to you because you belong to Him.

Walk with feisty faith today! He's got you.

The Lord your God in your midst,

The Mighty One, will save;

He will rejoice over you with gladness,

He will quiet you with His love,

He will rejoice over you with singing.

Zephaniah 3:17 NKJV

Heaven Rejoices Over You

May you—in spite of your critics—move forward in faith.

May God's song over your life drown out every lesser voice.

May you look up and rejoice because heaven rejoices over you.
Remember who you are today!

In Christ Jesus you possess all you need.

Your name is written on His hand.

Your desires are especially close to His heart.

His call on your life fits you perfectly.

Be watchful and thankful today.

Jesus is with you.

And Jabez called on the God of Israel saying, "Oh, that You would bless me indeed, and enlarge my territory, that Your hand would be with me, and that You would keep me from evil, that I may not cause pain!" So God granted him what he requested.

1 Chronicles 4:10 NKJV

Blessed in Every Way

May the Lord enlarge your territory, expand your influence, and increase your capacity to walk in faith.

May His hand of power be upon you in a way that marks everything you do.

May He keep you from harm   both causing and enduring it—and may He use you to bless a world very much in need.

May He surprise you with breakthroughs and still-water Sabbath moments.

Your Shepherd has placed His hand of blessing upon your head, and He will faithfully lead you.

Have a lighthearted, joy-filled day today!

The heavens declare the glory of God;

the skies proclaim the work of his hands.

Day after day they pour forth speech;

night after night they reveal knowledge.

PSALM 19:1–2

Ready for a Change

As the winds of change start to blow in your life, may you lean in and listen for the voice of the Lord.

Instead of looking for "signs" and mistakenly drawing the wrong conclusion, may you instead look to the Lord and His strength.

He'll speak to you in a way you'll understand.

God will lead you in the way you should go. He is faithful and true, and He's doing a NEW thing in your life!

Keep an ear bent toward heaven. Daily the heavens pour forth speech. May you listen for every word.

Blessings on your day today!

And that about wraps it up.

God is strong,

and he wants you strong.

EPHESIANS 6:10 THE MESSAGE

He Wants You Strong

May you remember today—above everything else—
that the One who put the stars in place greatly
delights in you. He is strong and powerful and
gentle and true.

Today, may you refuse to wonder if He cares, because
He truly, truly does.

May you soak in the reality of His presence and His love today.

May you read books, listen to music, and enjoy the company of
those who remind you who you are in Him; it'll strengthen your
soul!

And may you steward this day in
a way that replenishes you for the
journey ahead.

Have a great day.

What, then, shall we say
in response to these things?
If God is for us,
who can be against us?

Romans 8:31

Look Up and Sing

When you are tempted to look down in despair, may you instead look up and declare, "My God is for me, who can stand against me?"

When you are tempted to whine and grumble, may you instead dance and sing.

When you are tempted to gossip or be petty, may you instead pray and intercede.

God wants to bless the world through you!

Look up today and rejoice. All of heaven is on your side.

Praise the Lord, my soul; all my inmost being, praise his holy name. Praise the Lord, my soul, and forget not all his benefits—who forgives all your sins and heals all your diseases, who redeems your life from the pit and crowns you with love and compassion, who satisfies your desires with good things so that your youth is renewed like the eagle's.

Psalm 103:1–5

His Grace Strengthens You

May the Lord's grace and power make you bold and courageous.

May He remove from your midst sickness, despair, and disorder of every kind.

May He bring clarity, peace, and joy to your heart and mind.

And may your faith bring pleasure to His heart.

Have a great day!

Then will the eyes of the blind
be opened and the ears of the deaf
unstopped. Then will the lame leap like
a deer, and the mute tongue shout for joy.
Water will gush forth in the wilderness and
streams in the desert.

Isaiah 35:5–6

Believe for Greater Things

May you truly believe that God is up to something good in your life.

May the impossible suddenly seem possible.

May you envision the lost being found, the sick made well, and the poor made truly rich in Christ Jesus.

You are the object of God's great affection and provision.

You matter to Him more than you can comprehend.

Have a joy-filled day today.

Ah, Sovereign Lord,

you have made the heavens

and the earth by your great power

and outstretched arm.

Nothing is too hard for you.

JEREMIAH 32:17

God-Moments Everywhere

May salvation spring up all
around you!

May you see lives changed,
relationships restored, and bodies
healed everywhere you turn.

May your expectancy of what God can
and wants to do in your midst rise
exponentially.

He is a star-breathing, miracle-working,
intimately involved God.

Bless your day today.

The Lord himself goes before you

and will be with you;

he will never leave you nor forsake you.

Do not be afraid;

do not be discouraged.

DEUTERONOMY 31:8

Trust Him, He's Got You

May you rise up today with the full assurance that
God has your back.

He is with you, for you, and actively working on your behalf.

He does for you what you cannot do for yourself.

May you do for Him the one thing you can do: Trust Him with
your whole heart and embrace joy along the way.

Grace and peace to you this day!

Not that I have already obtained all this,
or have already arrived at my goal, but
I press on to take hold of that for which
Christ Jesus took hold of me. Brothers
and sisters, I do not consider myself yet
to have taken hold of it. But one thing
I do: Forgetting what is behind and
straining toward what is ahead, I press
on toward the goal to win the prize for
which God has called me heavenward in
Christ Jesus.

PHILIPPIANS 3:12–14

Embrace Today's Grace

May you refuse to drag the heavy baggage from your past another step.

May you refuse to borrow tomorrow's trouble when it's not yours to carry.

May you instead grab hold of today's mercy, today's grace, and today's power offered you right here, right now, for this moment.

May you walk in the delegated influence God has assigned you.

Walk in a manner worthy of His name.

And may holy confidence and humble dependence mark your life in every way today!

In their hearts humans plan their course,

but the Lord establishes their steps.

PROVERBS 16:9

Walk in Faith

May you—in spite of your fears—walk boldly
in faith.

May you know in the depths of your being how
"for you" God is!

May you embrace your sense of
purpose with tenacity and hope.

And may you walk so intimately with
God that He is able to divinely inter-
rupt your day whenever it suits Him.

Have a blessed, faith-filled day!

The Lord will guide you always;

he will satisfy your needs

in a sun-scorched land

and will strengthen your frame.

You will be like

a well-watered garden,

like a spring whose waters

never fail.

Isaiah 58:11

Fresh Favor and Perspective

May God Himself release fresh faith and perspective into your soul today!

May He strengthen your frame and establish your steps.

May He surround you with good friends who fear God and who love you.

May He give you fresh vision for your future and divine wisdom for stewarding your "now" moments.

May the song in your heart ring louder than the enemy's threats and accusations.

There is no one like our God and there is nothing like His love for you!

Walk blessed today, because you are!

Whoever believes in me,

as Scripture has said,

rivers of living water will flow

from within them.

John 7:38

A Glimpse of Glory

May God part the heavens and give you a glimpse of how
He sees you.

May He open up your eyes so you can see how much He
loves you.

May He awaken your soul so you'll know healing and
assurance like you've never known before. And may
His love pour in and through you like a river
of living water.

You're connected to the supernatural Source of
power—the Most High God.

May your understanding of what you possess in
Him increase exponentially today!

Dear friend,
I hope all is well with you
and that you are as healthy
in body as you are strong
in spirit.

3 John 1:2 NLT

Healed, Strong, and Whole

May Jesus Himself lift you up and make you strong.

May He heal those hidden areas that surface
time and time again.

May He bring wholeness and health to your mind, body,
and spirit.

May He strengthen you and fill you with faith so you'll dare
to take the risks He puts before you.

May you take time in His presence so you'll remember how
strong and mighty He is. And may your day be filled with
sacred moments that remind you just how precious
you are to Him.

You are so dear to His heart.

Don't worry about anything;
instead, pray about everything.
Tell God what you need,
and thank him for all he has done.
Then you will experience God's peace,
which exceeds anything
we can understand.
His peace will guard your hearts and
minds as you live in Christ Jesus.

PHILIPPIANS 4:6–7 NLT

Springtime Expectancy

May God Himself put springtime in your soul.

May you live today with expectancy that He's doing a new thing in your midst!

May you refuse worry, release your cares, and remember His promises. He'll make a way where there seems to be no way.

Have a faith-filled, expectant day today!

I place before you Life and Death,

Blessing and Curse.

Choose life so that you and your children

will live. And love God, your God,

listening obediently to him, firmly embracing

him. Oh yes, he is life itself,

a long life settled on the soil that God,

your God, promised to give your ancestors,

Abraham, Isaac, and Jacob.

DEUTERONOMY 30:19–20 THE MESSAGE

Choose Life

When the enemy tries to bait you into discouragement, may
you instead take your courageous stand in Christ Jesus.

When the devil tries to seduce you into despair, may
you instead walk through the door of hope God has
provided for you.

When you're tempted to walk down jealousy's
path, may you instead embrace your own beautiful
purpose and take the high road God has set
before you.

There's a best place for your feet today.

Choose life today!

Blessed is the one who
perseveres under trial because,
having stood the test,
that person will receive the crown of life
that the Lord has promised
to those who love him.

JAMES 1:12

Do Not Quit

May the Lord give you gritty perseverance
to stay the course and continue onward.

May He give you moments of
replenishment that refresh your soul
and renew your perspective.

May He use your wisdom and experience
to bless those who now walk where you've
walked. And may He inspire fresh faith to
trust Him in this place He has you.

You're blessed to be a blessing.

You're under His charge and under His care.

Walk on in faith today!

Consider it pure joy,

my brothers and sisters,

whenever you face trials of many kinds,

because you know that the testing of your faith

produces perseverance.

Let perseverance finish its work

so that you may be mature and complete,

not lacking anything.

JAMES 1:2–4

Joy and Strength

May God Himself fill you with pure joy amidst your trials.

May you understand that He's developing perseverance in you so you'll be mature and complete, lacking in nothing.

May you see the blessing in your battles.

Instead of becoming self-aware and wondering why so many arrows are aimed at you, may you simply become a better warrior.

May you lay hold of the generous amounts of wisdom God has offered you in this place so that when it's all said and done, you're still standing.

Have a great and victorious day.

Your love, Lord,

reaches to the heavens,

your faithfulness

to the skies.

Psalm 36:5

Confident in God

May your whole life align with God's best purposes for you!

May you pray in a way that reveals your solid belief in His faithfulness.

May you speak in a way that reflects the
power of His Word
mightily at work within you.

And may you walk on water when He bids you to come so that others will see and believe that God still moves on the earth today.

A blessed and faith-filled day to you!

She watches over the affairs

of her household and

does not eat the bread of idleness.

PROVERBS 31:27

Motivated and Purposeful

May you be motivated to exercise, organize, and prioritize.

May you embrace the grace to tend to the important things so they don't become urgent things.

May God bless you with focus, clarity, and inspiration to live an anointed and purposeful life starting today.

And may abundant grace and startling clarity be yours today!

"For I know the plans I have for you,"
declares the Lord, "plans to prosper you
and not to harm you, plans to give you hope
and a future. Then you will call on me
and come and pray to me, and I will listen
to you. You will seek me and find me
when you seek me with all your heart."

JEREMIAH 29:11–13

Remember and Dream With God

May you pause today, look back over your shoulder, and remember the ways God has been good to you, has come through for you, and has kept His word to you.

May you look ahead in faith with expectancy, as you get a sense of the land He wants you to claim.

May faith rise up within you as you take your first steps in that direction.

And may you embrace a renewed resolve to walk intimately with the One who loves you and has a beautiful plan for your life.

He deserves some sacred space in your day today!

Blessings to you.

Do not throw away
your confidence; it will be
richly rewarded.

HEBREWS 10:35

Breakthrough and Renewal

May your persistent prayers pay off and may the
burdens that have plagued you suddenly feel like a
light and easy yoke.

May this "suddenly" breakthrough come quickly.

May God grant you a fresh revelation of His love and
a fresh outpouring of grace to not only face the day but to conquer
it valiantly.

And may you experience increasing joy because you believe—
beyond a shadow of a doubt—that God has amazing things
planned for you! Have a GREAT day

For no word from God

will ever fail.

LUKE 1:37

Fresh, Unfailing Mercies

May God Himself wrap you up in His new mercies this day!

Where you've known angst, may He give you awe-inspiring wonder.

Where you've known heartbreak, may He bring healing, deliverance, and a supernatural breakthrough.

May He help you blow the dust off your dreams and lift them up as a possibility once again. With God all things are possible. May you learn to pray from that beautiful truth.

Be lifted up today. He's got you!

Come, let us sing for joy to the Lord;

let us shout aloud

to the Rock of our salvation.

Let us come before him

with thanksgiving and extol him

with music and song.

PSALM 95:1–2 NIV

Worship Wins the Day

May you awaken to the divine power of a grateful heart.

May you know there's victory in praise and breakthrough in thanksgiving!

When you stomp your feet, raise your hands, and sing a song of praise, the enemy scurries away, covers his ears, and his plans come to nothing.

With God on your side, you have all you need to win your battles and grow in love.

Sing a song of praise today even while you wait for your breakthrough!

A blessed day to you.

But he said to me,
"My grace is sufficient for you,
for my power is made perfect
in weakness." Therefore
I will boast all the more gladly
about my weaknesses,
so that Christ's power
may rest on me.

2 Corinthians 12:9

There's a Place for You

When you feel like you don't fit in, may you walk in faith because you have a place at the Table of Grace.

When you feel like you're just not enough, may you remember that His Enough is more than enough for you.

When you trip up and fall short, remember that He stoops down to make you great.

And when you don't feel victorious, remember that you're already seated with Christ because He won the victory for you.

Have a great day!

It is good to praise the Lord

and make music to your name,

O Most High, proclaiming your love

in the morning

and your faithfulness at night.

PSALM 92:1–2

Prayer Changes Things

May you begin to see with Spirit eyes all the ways God is moving because of your prayers.

May you begin to hear with heavenly ears the song heaven sings over you.

May you begin to know—on a deeper level—how important and precious your faith is to God.

And may you begin to know that God's promises are absolutely true, and live accordingly.

You couldn't be more loved if you tried. He's sold on you.

A happy and blessed day to you!

I pray that you, being rooted and
established in love, may have power,
together with all the Lord's holy people,
to grasp how wide and long and high
and deep is the love of Christ,
and to know this love that surpasses
knowledge—that you may be filled
to the measure of all the fullness of God.

Ephesians 3:17–19

Filled to Overflowing

May you experience increase in every way.

May your capacity to know the heights of God's love grow exponentially.

May your understanding of the depths of His faithfulness grow continually.

May your belief in your divine value deepen tremendously.

And, in the days ahead, may your willingness to trust God with every detail of your life change profoundly.

You are deeply loved, deeply called, and profoundly cared for. May you live out of this truth!

Walk in humble confidence today.

Now you have every
spiritual gift you need
as you eagerly wait for
the return of our Lord Jesus Christ.
He will keep you strong to the end
so that you will be free
from all blame on the day
when our Lord Jesus Christ returns.

1 Corinthians 1:7–8 NLT

Free to Be You

May you find a new freedom in being the YOU God created you to be!

May you be comfortable in your own skin, excited about your own story, and at peace with your own past because Christ has redeemed every part of you.

May you break free from condemnation, may you walk away from toxic influences, and may you put fear under your feet.

Let faith fill your heart. Do not give people the power that belongs to God alone.

He loves you.

He is strong.

And He'll keep you strong till the end.

Have a faith-filled day today!

So we fix our eyes not on what is seen,

but on what is unseen,

since what is seen is temporary,

but what is unseen is eternal.

2 Corinthians 4:18

Release Your Cares

May God Himself surround you with His tender mercies and grace today.

May He heal your soul so you can live by faith.

Where you once reacted out of your insecurities, may you respond in faith knowing you possess all in Christ.

Where you once white-knuckled your worries, may you release every care to Him and lift your hands in praise.

You are not made for this world. You are only passing through.

Live as the divinely loved and called soul you are!

May the God of hope fill you with all joy
and peace as you trust in him,
so that you may overflow with hope
by the power of the Holy Spirit.

ROMANS 15:13

Simplify and Refresh

May God inspire you to tackle a project you've been putting off.

May He motivate you to clean out the clutter and simplify your surroundings.

May He refresh your weary soul and renew your tired mind. And in every way, may your soul be restored, your mind renewed, and your spirit at peace.

He leads you by still waters; follow Him there.

Be revived and refreshed this day!

Give, and it will be given to you.

A good measure, pressed down,

shaken together and running over,

will be poured into your lap.

For with the measure you use,

it will be measured to you.

Luke 6:38

Sow Generously

May you choose joy this day!

May you look for and count your many blessings.

May you sow generously for a future harvest.

May you trust God with the seeds you have in the ground.

And may you add faith to every deed, knowing that God multiplies what we sow in faith.

Have an abundantly joyful day today!

Blessed are the meek,

for they will inherit the earth.

MATTHEW 5:5

Humility and Tenacity

May God fill you with strength and power to embrace His grace this very hour.

May you humble yourself before Him so that He may lift you up and bless you before a watching world.

May you embrace a humble, teachable heart while maintaining tenacious and ferocious faith.

May you bow low when He speaks and rise up when He tells you to move.

Our God is King, and He moves mightily in and through His people.

Live expectantly today!

He got up, rebuked the wind
and said to the waves, "Quiet! Be still!"
Then the wind died down and
it was completely calm.

MARK 4:39

Peace to Your Storm

May Jesus speak peace to your soul and calm to your storm.

May you sense His nearness even when the winds blow.

May you know His joy and strength from the top of your head to the tips your toes.

May the hope He stirs in your heart cause you to live with a holy expectancy and trust that this storm too shall pass.

And in the days ahead, may His very real love for you compel you to dance in the rain before the sun breaks through.

Jesus goes before you, He's got your back, and He's there, just around the bend.

He'll never forsake you.

Trust Him today!

Every valley shall be raised up,

every mountain and hill made low;

the rough ground shall become level,

the rugged places a plain.

And the glory of the Lord will be revealed,

and all people will see it together.

For the mouth of the Lord has spoken.

ISAIAH 40:4–5

Seated With Christ

No matter if you're in the valley or on a mountain, may you remember most importantly that as a Christ-follower you are seated with Christ in the heavenly realms.

Everything He has is yours.

He has written your name on His hand and holds your desires close to His heart.

Though the elements rage on earth, your footing is secure in Him.

Stay hidden in the shelter of His wing; stay in that place of peace.

May you remember today that nothing can separate you from His powerful, personal love for you.

You're everything to Him.

My salvation and my honor

depend on God;

he is my mighty rock,

my refuge.

PSALM 62:7

Forgiveness and Mercy

May God overwhelm you with grace to forgive those who've hurt you, to forgive yourself for hurting others, and to release the outcomes into His hands.

May He give you the peace to walk forward surrounded by His mercy and held up by His love.

May you look forward expectantly with hope and anticipation because God has the wisdom and the power to make things right.

He redeems, restores, and makes all things new.

Have a great, hope-filled day!

Teach me to do your will,

for you are my God;

may your good Spirit lead me

on level ground.

PSALM 143:10

Don't Give Up

If you're in a situation you don't want to be in, may you find new strength to stand strong and new resolve to keep walking.

May you earnestly seek God in this place.

May you continue to ask for His strength, insight, and intervention in your life.

May you embrace the expectancy that any day now, your breakthrough will come.

Don't give up hope.

He's got you and you have Him.

You're in this together.

A blessed, faith-filled day to you today!

But the Lord is with me

like a mighty warrior;

so my persecutors will stumble

and not prevail.

They will fail and be thoroughly disgraced;

their dishonor will never be forgotten.

JEREMIAH 20:11

Hold Your Ground

In the face of the enemy's lies, taunts, and threats, may you tighten your belt of truth, raise your shield of faith, and hold your ground.

May you refuse to be bullied by your fears or pushed around by your past mistakes.

May you instead look to Jesus, the Author and Finisher of your faith.

May you dare to look ahead to the promised land He's offered you.

You are equipped to win your fear-battle, so press in and press on today!

"The glory of this present house
will be greater than the glory of
the former house,"
says the Lord Almighty.
"And in this place I will grant peace."

HAGGAI 2:9

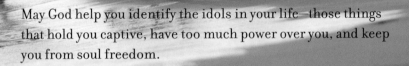

Break Free

May God help you identify the idols in your life—those things that hold you captive, have too much power over you, and keep you from soul freedom.

May you give God the glory He deserves.

May you ascribe to Him the power you once gave to others.

May you thank Him for the future the enemy has threatened to steal from you.

May you walk forward with abundant grace, divine peace, and overwhelming joy because you're profoundly rich in Christ.

Shake the shackles off your feet and praise Him! He's set you free today and every day!

He put a new song in my mouth,

a hymn of praise to our God.

Many will see and fear the Lord

and put their trust in him.

Psalm 40:3

Spacious Places

May the God of all comfort surround you with His tender mercies and strength.

May He breathe fresh life into your soul and put a new song in your heart.

May He broaden the path beneath your feet and make your footsteps firm.

And may He lead you to a spacious place and answer your heartfelt prayers.

A blessed and beautiful day to you this day!

I'm absolutely convinced that nothing—nothing living or dead, angelic or demonic, today or tomorrow, high or low, thinkable or unthinkable—absolutely nothing can get between us and God's love because of the way that Jesus our Master has embraced us.

ROMANS 8:38–39
THE MESSAGE

He Loves and He Restores

May God Himself recover and restore
what the enemy has stolen.

May He heal family rifts, renew tired relationships, and revive
weary faith.

May He lift you up and make you strong.

May He give you wisdom in boundaries and humility in love.

May He show you what's yours and give you grace
to release what isn't.

And may you know beyond a shadow of a doubt that
nothing and no one can separate you from God's love.

Walk in humble, hopeful faith today.

Turn my eyes away from
worthless things;
preserve my life according to
your word.

PSALM 119:37

A Fresh Outpouring

May God unleash a
fresh outpouring of
His grace and goodness
over your life.

May He open heaven's doors and
pour out His Spirit in increasing measures.

May He firmly establish you in His highest
and best purposes for you.

May you acquire such a taste for the presence
of God that you're no longer tempted
or distracted by cheap counterfeits and
temporary sources.

He is the one true God and He delights in every
detail of your life.

Have a blessed, power-full day!

He who was seated on the throne said,

"I am making everything new!"

Then he said,

"Write this down, for these words

are trustworthy and true."

REVELATION 21:5

God Is Doing a New Thing

May God do a brand-new thing in and through you!

May He break every generational stronghold that
keeps you from knowing and experiencing His great
love for you.

May He move every mountain that blocks your
view of Him.

May He fill every low place with pools of blessing.

And may He restore everything stolen so you
can have the life He intended for you from the
beginning of time.

Your Redeemer is strong and mighty and loves
you deeply.

Live joyfully today!

Go, walk through the length
and breadth of the land,
for I am giving it to you.

GENESIS 13:17

Your Next Place of Promise

May the Lord remove every distraction that keeps you from the land He has for you.

May you walk forward in faith to possess it.

May you trust His process as He prepares you to dwell in that land so you can feed on His faithfulness.

Your current battles are training you not only to take the land, but to stand there, fight there, win there, and be fruitful there!

The Lord your God is with you!

Here is my servant, whom I uphold,

my chosen one in whom I delight;

I will put my Spirit on him,

and he will bring justice to the nations.

Isaiah 42:1

See Yourself Through His Eyes

May God open your Spirit eyes to see your life, your worth, and your destiny from His point of view.

He's doing a beautiful work in you!

May you open wide your arms and receive His abundant love, His powerful promises, and His moment-by-moment faithfulness.

He will not fail you!

May you live as one who is spoken for, provided for, and deeply loved.

Because you are.

Have a great day!

Therefore, my dear brothers and
sisters, stand firm.
Let nothing move you.
Always give yourselves fully to
the work of the Lord,
because you know that your labor
in the Lord is not in vain.

1 Corinthians 15:58

God Is in Control

May you be assured on a whole new level of how much God loves you and that He's constantly working on your behalf.

May you feel a fresh surge of confidence amidst your circumstances because you know that God is ultimately in control, and nothing escapes His notice.

He only allows battles you can win, and in every one there are treasures and spoils with your name on them.

Live bravely today!

Lord my God,

I called to you for help,

and you healed me.

PSALM 30:2

Give Him Access to You

May you give God full access
to your story.

May you allow Him to
correct and redirect,
heal and deal, refine and
define, whenever it suits
Him.

He loves you most and
knows what's best for
you at every given moment.
He will lead you in the way you
should go.

May you remember that you're part of
a great story God is writing in the world.

May you trust the Lord's work in your life so He can
use you in ways beyond your wildest dreams.

Lean in and trust Him. He's got you.

Then Job replied to the
Lord: "I know that you
can do all things; no purpose
of yours can be thwarted.
You asked, 'Who is this that
obscures my plans without
knowledge?' Surely I spoke of
things I did not understand,
things too wonderful
for me to know."

Job 42:1–3

Unshakable

In this day of uncertainty, may God give you a faith that cannot be shaken.

When all is in chaos, may you have divine clarity to see God's highest will and divine movement all around you.

May you know peace that passes understanding and pass it on to others.

Stand strong, my friend!

You possess all in Him.

Walk forward unafraid.

Therefore, if anyone is in Christ, the new creation has come: The old has gone, the new is here! All this is from God, who reconciled us to himself through Christ and gave us the ministry of reconciliation.

2 CORINTHIANS 5:17–18

The New You

May you refuse an anxious heart and embrace a faith-filled one.

May you stomp on your fears and dance because of your dreams.

May you shun the shame of your youth and hold tight your new identity in Christ.

You are not an improved version of your old self. You are something altogether new, profoundly beautiful, and abundantly equipped.

Walk fully in the blessing and purposes of God today.

Why, my soul, are you downcast?

Why so disturbed within me?

Put your hope in God,

for I will yet praise him,

my Savior and my God.

PSALM 42:5

Trust Him Fully

May you dare to trust in the Lord with your whole heart and not lean on your own understanding.

May you look up and acknowledge Him with every step you take, knowing He'll get you where you need to go.

May you put your hope in Him and not in the approval of man.

God will never disappoint.

He loves you more than you can comprehend.

Trust Him, and soon your eyes will see how good He is.

Blessings on your day today!

Curses chase sinners
while blessings chase
the righteous!

PROVERBS 13:21 TLB

Abundantly Blessed

May abundant grace and profound peace be multiplied to you in every way.

May countless blessings chase and overtake you, and may you notice when they do.

May God heal your heart, soul, mind, and body, and may you approach life with eternity in mind.

May you know the wholeness God always intended for you, and may your faith be renewed.

Look for Him expectantly today!

Every good and perfect gift

is from above,

coming down from the Father

of the heavenly lights,

who does not change like

shifting shadows.

JAMES 1:17

A Playful Moment

May you face today with
a smile and with hopeful
expectancy.

May God surprise you with a
song that speaks to your heart.

May you enjoy a sudden playful
moment and enter in with your
whole heart.

And may you notice that every good
gift in your life comes from
above.

In every season, He gives good
gifts to His children.

A blessed and wonderful day to
you this day!

Be completely humble
and gentle;
be patient,
bearing with one another
in love.

EPHESIANS 4:2

Energized and Purposeful

May God infuse you with divine energy and purpose today.

May He fuel your prayers and sanctify your words.

May He open your eyes to see evidences of His handiwork
everywhere you turn.

And may He connect you with people you need to meet,
people who need your blessing.

Step forward with authority, confidence, joy, and
strength today.

You are mighty in God!

I pray that out of his glorious riches

he may strengthen you with power

through his Spirit

in your inner being.

Ephesians 3:16

Keep Walking

May you dare to keep walking even though quitting feels like the easier thing to do.

May you dare to look up even though the weight of your burden compels you to look down.

May you dare to dream about the future even though the enemy would love for your past to have the last say.

Keep walking, look up, and dare to dream.

Jesus invites you forward.

Embrace joy today, and don't give up!

But you have

God-blessed eyes—eyes that see!

And God-blessed ears—ears that hear!

A lot of people, prophets and

humble believers among them,

would have given anything to see

what you are seeing, to hear

what you are hearing,

but never had the chance.

MATTHEW 13:16–17 THE MESSAGE

A Heart Like His

May you be so aware of God's love that you
live as one who is spoken for.

May you be so in tuned to His voice that the
kingdom of God comes everywhere you
place your feet.

May you be so moved by His loving
heart for the least and the lost that
you're quick to see them, quick to
reach them.

And may you be so profoundly aware of
God's song over your life that it puts a
spring in your step.

Walk blessed today.

You matter deeply to God.

Guard my life,

for I am faithful to you;

save your servant who trusts in you.

You are my God.

PSALM 86:2

Wisdom to Guard and Guide

May God be exalted in your life today!

May He surround you with fresh mercies and fiery faith, and may His divine wisdom guard and guide you.

May you refuse to dabble in things that make you vulnerable to the enemy's schemes.

May you instead shore up your life, guard your heart, and walk in faith.

You've a great call on your life, and the Lord is mighty in you and through you!

And we know that in all things
God works for the good of those
who love him,
who have been called
according to his purpose.

ROMANS 8:28

Awaken Your Faith

May God ignite fresh faith in you today!

May you pray with clarity, precision, and power.

May you stand on His Word and hold fast to His promises.

May you refuse to fixate on your difficulties, and instead fix your eyes on Jesus—the One who will finish what He started in you.

He is always good, always kind, always true, and He WILL come through for you!

May the Lord overwhelm you with an awakening of faith, hope, and love today.

Look up and be blessed.

Then Peter called to him,
"Lord, if it's really you,
tell me to come to you,
walking on the water."

MATTHEW 14:28 NLT

Say Yes

May Jesus bring clarity to His future plans for you.

May you suddenly be assured on a much greater level of
His deep love for you and of His intimate attention to detail.

As He bids you to come, may you let go of what feels safe
to lay hold of the new place He has for you.

He's doing a new thing; don't hang on to the old just because
you know it so well—don't miss out on the invitation.

Take the next faith step in front of you, and have a blessed
and beautiful day!

For we live by believing,

not by seeing.

2 CORINTHIANS 5:7 NLT

Believe, Then See

May you walk by faith and not by sight.

May you live by the promises of God and not by what your eyes see.

May you—even today—see movement in your circumstances, glimpses of glory that remind you your God is very much involved in your life.

He's writing a story, arranging circumstances, moving in the hearts of people specifically for you. He loves you that much.

Let your joyful heart testify to your abounding trust in Him. It'll please God and encourage others!

He makes me lie down in green pastures,

he leads me beside quiet waters,

he refreshes my soul.

He guides me along the right paths

for his name's sake.

Psalm 23:2–3

Still Waters

May the Lord lead you beside still waters and restore your soul.

May He refresh your sense of purpose.

May He renew your love for those He's given to you.

And may He stir in you a hunger to know Him more.

He's only a prayer away.

Embrace a heart at rest this day.

Be still, and know that I am God;

I will be exalted among the nations,

I will be exalted in the earth.

PSALM 46:10

He's With You

May the Lord reveal His goodness and kindness today.

May you enjoy an intimate and personal relationship with Him. He's right here, with you, and for you.

When you start to strive, may you instead pause, look up, and acknowledge His presence in your life. You're never alone; never out of His care.

Everything He has is yours. You lack no good thing.

Walk in faith today.

May God himself, the God of peace,

sanctify you through and through.

May your whole spirit, soul and body be kept

blameless at the coming of our

Lord Jesus Christ.

The one who calls you is faithful,

and he will do it.

1 Thessalonians 5:23–24

In Step With Him

May you be so in tune with the Holy Spirit's movement in your life that you're always in the right place at the right time.

May your every step be ordered by the Lord.

May you go where He'd have you go, say what He'd have you say, and pray what He'd have you pray.

May you be a vessel that Jesus fills up and pours out on a dry and thirsty land.

And may your own soul be re-plenished in the process.

Have a great day today!

Surely, Lord,
you bless the righteous;
you surround them with your
favor as with a shield.

Psalm 5:12

Surrounded With Favor

May God surround you with His favor as with a shield.

May you walk with humble confidence knowing
that you have everything you need because you
have Him.

May your eyes of faith help you see what you
cannot see on your own.

May your sense of God's purpose keep you moving
forward.

And may He anoint you to walk through life totally
and completely transformed.

God is on your side.

Heal me, Lord, and I will be healed;

save me and I will be saved,

for you are the one I praise.

JEREMIAH 17:14

Satisfied and Strengthened

May the Lord strengthen your frame and heal your soul.

May He satisfy your needs in a sun-scorched land.

May you receive all He so lovingly pours out on you and become like a well-watered garden, like a spring whose waters never fail.

And may many be nourished by your life and come to know Jesus more intimately because of your healed, whole life.

Live full of faith and free in Him today!

For the Lord God is a sun and shield;

the Lord bestows favor and honor;

no good thing does he withhold from

those whose walk is blameless.

Psalm 84:11

His Goodness

May you focus more on Jesus' goodness than on your badness.

May you get excited about His supply instead of despairing over what you lack in yourself.

May you look to Him and imagine what's possible instead of looking down at what seems impossible.

God is doing a new thing in your midst.

Lean in and look for Him with expectancy today, for every good gift comes from Him and He loves His children deeply.

Choose joy this day!

Be strong and take heart,

all you who hope in the Lord.

PSALM 31:24

Be Strong, Take Heart

May you refuse to connect the dots on your painful experiences and thus draw a wrong conclusion about yourself and God.

May you instead be hemmed in by God's powerful promises, and may you be defined by His very personal love for you.

May you refuse to let your past speak to you, except to teach you.

And may you insist on living as one who has a redemptive story to tell. You are that important to God's kingdom-story.

Walk assured today.

God is with you.

God can do anything, you know—
far more than you could ever imagine
or guess or request in your wildest dreams!
He does it not by pushing us around
but by working within us,
his Spirit deeply and gently within us.

EPHESIANS 3:20 THE MESSAGE

A Divinely Paced Life

May you suddenly grow in your capacity to understand
God's love.

May the reality of His feelings toward you put your heart
at ease and fill your soul with gladness.

May the rush and worry culture have no impact on you.

And may the Lord Himself set your pace and
establish you in your purpose.

His yoke is precious, beautiful, divine,
and doable.

Peace to you.

Above all else,

guard your heart,

for everything you do

flows from it.

PROVERBS 4:23

Guard Your Heart

May you guard your heart from toxic influences.

May you steward your times of rest so they will truly replenish you.

May you cast down every negative, defeating thought that sets itself above the knowledge and goodness of God.

And may you give the Lord His rightful place in your life: above your fears, above your worries, and above your frustrations.

He is God Most High, and when He reigns in your life, you will thrive.

Be blessed this day!

And I ask him that with both feet planted
firmly on love, you'll be able to take in
with all followers of Jesus the extravagant
dimensions of Christ's love. Reach out
and experience the breadth! Test its length!
Plumb the depths! Rise to the heights!
Live full lives, full in the fullness of God.

EPHESIANS 3:17–19 THE MESSAGE

Receive, Believe, Live

As you breathe in the morning air, may you breathe in a fresh revelation of God's love.

As you stretch your muscles and move through your day, may you also activate and stretch your faith in the promises of God.

Believe God when He says He is for you and with you.

You possess more than you need when you are in Christ Jesus.

Walk, live, and breathe like the heir of God you are.

Be dressed ready for service
and keep your lamps burning.

LUKE 12:35

Ready to Respond

May God fill you afresh with His Spirit
so that you will respond in faith to the
smallest nudge within you.

May you walk away from time wasters so that
you may possess all God longs to give you.

May you turn a deaf ear to lies that "feel
true" so you can embrace the beautiful
truth that is true!

And may God's presence and love be
tangible to you today.

Do not be afraid, for I have ransomed you.

I have called you by name; you are mine.

When you go through deep waters,

I will be with you.

When you go through rivers of difficulty,

you will not drown.

Isaiah 43:1–2 NLT

Do Not Fear

When you can't sense what God is up to, may you trust even more His heart toward you.

When your journey is different than you would choose, may you see His invitation to make you new.

When the storm rages overhead, may you know—with everything in you—that new mercies are on the other side.

And when you're tempted to overstate your problems and understate His promises, may you step back and find your footing again.

On Christ the solid Rock you stand, all other ground is sinking sand.

Embrace a joy-perspective this day!

Commit to the Lord

whatever you do,

and he will establish your plans.

PROVERBS 16:3

God Will Move

May you throw aside your
detailed expectations of
what you want others to
do for you, and throw
your arms open with fresh
expectancy that God will
move in His time and
His way according to His
wisdom and will.

He is your source of life
and will never let you down
or forsake you.

You possess all when you have Him.

Bless your precious, faith-filled heart today!

I pray that the eyes of your heart

may be enlightened in order that

you may know the hope

to which he has called you,

the riches of his glorious

inheritance in his holy people.

 EPHESIANS 1:18

What's Best for Your Soul

May God divinely motivate you to do what's best for your soul.

If it's spring cleaning, may you clean with a new song in your heart.

If it's reading a book, may you find one that rocks your world.

If it's sharing what you've learned, may you speak with God's passion and power.

And if it's giving, may you give generously and joyfully, believing God will resupply and then some.

Your journey is unique to you.

Listen for His voice and do what He says. God's best is your best!

I desire to do your will,

my God;

your law is within my heart.

PSALM 40:8

Live in Response to Him

May you refuse the autopilot life.

May you instead be a lean-in-and-listen kind of person.

May you be quick to discern the Lord's whisper and quick to follow His lead.

May you notice the winds of change
blowing in the trees and loosen
your tent stakes if the Lord
requires it.

And may you
cup your ear toward
heaven and treasure the Lord's voice above all others.

Enjoy your day today!

Blessed are those who fear the Lord,

who find great delight in his commands.

Their children will be mighty in the land;

the generation of the upright

will be blessed.

PSALM 112:1–2

He Loves Your Loved Ones

May you learn to rest in the goodness of God.

When you're tempted to worry about your loved ones, may you instead rejoice that your Savior runs after them with an earnest love, deep compassion, and profound wisdom. He longs to be gracious to them and show them His lovingkindness.

May you feel free to exhale your worries and breathe in His promises because they are true and they're for you.

It's time to refuse angst and remember that He is God, He is good, and He cares about every detail of your life.

Walk blessed today because you are!

For the Spirit God gave us
does not make us timid,
but gives us power, love
and self-discipline.

2 Timothy 1:7

He'll Empower You

May God Himself lift you up and encourage you today!

Where you're weary, may He revive and replenish you.

Where you're discouraged, may He infuse strength.

Where you're feeling snarky, may He calm you and make you gracious.

And where you're afraid, may He fill you with faith.

Life is hard but God is good, and He is with you every step of the way, today and every day!

Nehemiah said, "Go and enjoy choice food and sweet drinks, and send some to those who have nothing prepared. This day is holy to our Lord. Do not grieve, for the joy of the Lord is your strength."

NEHEMIAH 8:10

Bursts of Joy

May God give you a burst of energy to tackle the tasks that you need to get done.

May He inspire you to turn up the radio and dance in your kitchen.

May He fill you with such joy that you suddenly realize just how rich you really are.

May He connect you with an old friend and bless you with a new friend.

And may He use you in surprising ways to be a blessing to everyone you meet today.

Have a bursting-with-joy day today!

See, I have engraved you

on the palms of my hands;

your walls are ever before me.

Isaiah 49:16

You're Someone He Loves

May you know in your core being
that you are not defined by your past
mistakes.

May you humbly understand that nei-
ther are you defined by your accumulated
achievements.

You are someone God loves.

You bear the image of the Most High God.

Your name is written on His hand; your
desires are close to His heart.

The fact that you're on the heart and
mind of almighty God is what makes you
a priceless, worthwhile treasure.

Live life according to the fullness
of that truth.

I keep asking that the God of
our Lord Jesus Christ, the glorious Father,
may give you the Spirit of wisdom
and revelation, so that you
may know him better.

EPHESIANS 1:17

Know Him More

May Jesus stir up in you a fresh hunger and passion to know
Him more intimately.

May He give you a gift of faith that swallows up your fears.

May He plant a dream in your soul that fits you perfectly.

And may He show you the sacred path you must take to
lay hold of it.

Have a blessed and restful day!

In the Messiah, in Christ,
God leads us from place to place
in one perpetual victory parade.
Through us, he brings knowledge
of Christ. Everywhere we go,
people breathe in the
exquisite fragrance.

2 CORINTHIANS 2:14 THE MESSAGE

Before the Breakthrough Comes

May God give you extra grace to thrive even when your heart is breaking.

May you enjoy spilling-over-joy even before the breakthrough comes.

May you find cause to celebrate and rejoice over all that is right in your world.

Refuse to let worry have the last say.

God is the Redeemer and makes all things new.

Never give up hope.

May you dare to believe that your latter days may be more blessed than your former days.

Walk in faith today.

I wait for the Lord,

my whole being waits,

and in his word

I put my hope.

PSALM 130:5

Any Day Now

May you become powerful in God as you wait for your breakthrough. In this "not yet" season, may you learn the secret of abiding in Him.

May you send your roots down into His marvelous love, and instinctively trust that He has your absolute best in mind.

May you be so acquainted with His Word and His presence that you—right here, right now—plant seeds of faith for a future harvest.

Instead of angst over your "not yet," may you embrace awe for the reality of your faith, the substance of His promises, and the surety that any day now HE WILL BREAK THROUGH!

In your unfailing love,

silence my enemies;

destroy all my foes,

for I am your servant.

Psalm 143:12

Treasures in the Valley

If you're walking through a dark valley, may you hear God's promise to you: "I will give you treasures in this valley! Riches stored in secret places!"

May you walk forward unafraid and full of faith that He'll fill your arms with spoils from this war and treasures to share with others who need what you'll learn.

Be strong and take heart.

God is near even if you can't feel Him.

He's for you, with you, and making a way where there is no way.

Don't give up. You'll be richer for the battle.

Blessings on your day today!

The Lord will indeed give
what is good, and our land
will yield its harvest.

PSALM 85:12 NIV

Pray, Plant, and Believe

May you understand—on a whole new level—
how much God is for you.

May you see wonders unfold before you that
remind you how much it matters that you pray.

May you plant new seeds of faith, expectant that
you'll see a harvest in the days to come.

May you take a few faith steps today even if you
don't feel like it.

And may you invite God to heal a deep soul wound that
has plagued you for far too long.

It's a new season.

Be strong in the Lord!

He will yet fill your mouth with laughter
and your lips with shouts of joy.

JOB 8:21

Surprised by Joy

May God surprise you today with oasis moments of refreshment and encouragement.

May He delight your heart with a kind and unexpected word.

May He use you to be a source of refreshment to many.

And may you pause today to notice the good things in your life, and give thanks.

You are blessed and loved, and you have access to a divine supply you could never exhaust or use up.

Be present in the moment and trust God to give you what you need.

Receive and experience
the amazing grace of the Master,
Jesus Christ, deep,
deep within yourselves.

PHILIPPIANS 4:23 THE MESSAGE

Receive!

May you lift your head, open your arms, and receive all God so lovingly wants to pour into you today.

May you shake off the cloak of discouragement and leave it on the ground where it belongs.

God is doing a new thing in your midst!

He's already at work on your behalf.

Do not fix your mind on the things that frustrate you or break your heart.

Fix your eyes on the Author and Finisher of your faith, who will complete what He started!

Walk with faith and hope and love today!

Rejoice always, pray continually,
give thanks in all circumstances;
for this is God's will for you
in Christ Jesus.

1 Thessalonians 5:16–18

Pray Powerfully

May God revive your heart for earnest, consistent prayer.

May you remember once again that God moves on every act prompted by your faith.

May you rejoice in the fact that God keeps His promises and answers prayers.

Even though you can't see it yet, Jesus has created a stream in the desert for you. He's made a way where there's been no way. And soon you will see the breakthrough.

So rejoice today!

Pray today!

Believe today!

After they prayed,

the place where they were meeting

was shaken.

And they were all filled with the Holy Spirit

and spoke the word of God boldly.

ACTS 4:31

God Is Near

May God's Spirit stir up your faith and quicken your heart
so you sense His nearness like never before.

May His power mark your life, the way you pray,
and what you say.

May His love fill you and spill out of you to the broken
and hurting souls in your midst.

As you delight deeply in Him, may He overwhelm
you with the deep desires of your heart.

Worship Him passionately today!

Come to me, all you who
are weary and burdened,
and I will give you rest.
Take my yoke upon you and learn
from me, for I am gentle and humble in
heart, and you will find rest for your souls.
For my yoke is easy
and my burden is light.

MATTHEW 11:28–30

Rest While He Works

May the phrase "Let go and let God" take on a whole new meaning for you.

May you learn to rest while He works on your behalf.

May you understand your role in this kingdom-story and do only what He tells you to do.

May you live free from the bondage of others' opinions so you're free to love them the way Christ does.

And may others be so drawn to your healed heart that they come to know Jesus for themselves.

Rest in Him.

Forget the former things;

do not dwell on the past.

See, I am doing a new thing!

Now it springs up;

do you not perceive it?

I am making a way in the wilderness

and streams in the wasteland.

ISAIAH 43:18–19

Rest, Revival, and Renewal

May this next season for you be one of rest, revival, and renewal.

May you experience the REST of God in your most trying circumstances, and as a result, find peace and bear fruit where there's only been angst and thorns.

May you experience a personal REVIVAL that changes how you pray, what you say, and where you put your time.

And may you experience such soul RENEWAL that even the old things in your life feel new.

God doesn't make things "nice," He makes things new.

Trust Him to do a brand-new work in you in the days ahead.

You did not choose me,

but I chose you and appointed you

so that you might go and bear fruit—

fruit that will last—and so that whatever

you ask in my name

the Father will give you.

This is my command:

Love each other.

John 15:16–17

Divinely Called

May you begin to see your disappointments as divine appointments.

May your Spirit eyes open up to God's invitation to something better, something deeper, something profoundly fitted for you.

May you lift your eyes and see how your whole story fits in the bigger story God is writing for His Namesake.

God intends to solve some of the world's problems through you.

Trust Him and let Him use you in ways that are beyond you!

Look for those appointments, and have a great day.

Blessings for Specific Needs and Occasions

Let my soul be at rest again, for
the Lord has been good to me.

PSALM 116:7 NLT

A Restful Weekend

May you have time this weekend to pause, be still, and to dream with God.

What does He have for you in the days ahead?

May you move the clutter out of the way and make room for Jesus to change your life and establish you in His purposes for you.

May the constant flurried activity be replaced by memories of how God has come through for you and absolute clarity about the things He has for you in the future.

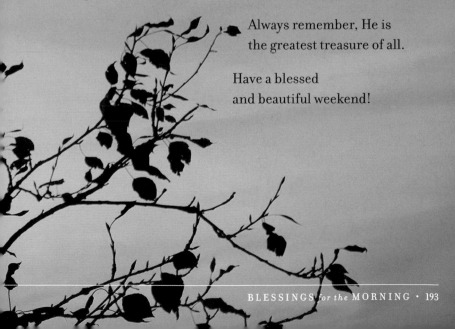

Always remember, He is the greatest treasure of all.

Have a blessed and beautiful weekend!

By faith Abraham, when called
to go to a place he would later receive
as his inheritance, obeyed and went,
even though he did not know
where he was going.

HEBREWS 11:8

Stepping Out in Faith

May you have the holy inspiration to live up to what you already know!

As you wait on God for your marching orders, may you fully believe that He'll supply your every need.

May you become a bold, brave warrior who stands in faith, trusts wholeheartedly, and testifies to what God has done.

May your life be marked by power, authority, and mostly love.

And may the reality of Christ in you mark your life in every way, so that wherever you place your feet, God's kingdom comes to earth.

There is now
no condemnation
for those who are in
Christ Jesus.

Romans 8:1

No Condemnation

May you refuse to drag your past with you another step.

May you stop right here, stomp your feet, and raise your hands in the air because Christ has set you free!

He has redeemed you, received you, and claimed you for His purposes! He has forgiven you and filled you anew with His powerful Holy Spirit.

There is NOW no condemnation for you because you are in Him and He is in you!

Walk free and full of grace—even amidst your weaknesses and frailties—because He's got you. You are one of the good gifts He offers to a world very much in need.

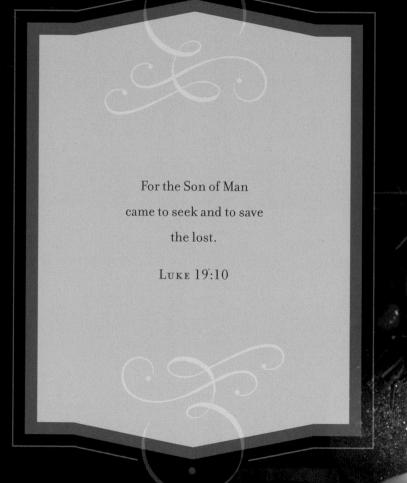

For the Son of Man
came to seek and to save
the lost.

LUKE 19:10

Christmas Eve

May the wonder of Christ's very personal love for you overwhelm you and make your knees weak.

May the reality that He came to earth to seek and save the lost give you a heart for those who've lost their way .

May the power of His Spirit within you compel you to walk by faith and not by sight. May the promise of His unconditional love compel you to dream big, take risks, and give generously.

As you wrap up this year, may you wear His grace like a beautiful robe, may you entrust your missteps to Him, and may you trust Him to transform you from the inside out.

A very blessed and merry Christmas to you!

But the angel said to them,

"Do not be afraid. I bring you good news

that will cause great joy for all the people.

Today in the town of David

a Savior has been born to you;

he is the Messiah,

the Lord."

Luke 2:10–11

Christmas

May you pause for a moment
today and consider this:
YOU are the object of God's
affection.

YOU are the reason Jesus came
to earth as vulnerable baby.

YOU were the joy set before Him
when He endured the cross and scorned
its shame.

Jesus made a public spectacle of the enemy that stands against
you; He crushed the lies the enemy spews about you because
YOU are someone Jesus loves and wants forever in eternity
with Him.

Jesus IS the reason for the season.

May we joyfully celebrate the One who came as a baby and will
return as the King.

Have a most blessed, festive day today!

For I am about to do something new.
See, I have already begun! Do you not
see it? I will make a pathway through
the wilderness. I will create rivers in
the dry wasteland.

ISAIAH 43:19 NLT

End of Year

As the year wraps up and draws to a close, may you let go of any lies you picked up along the way.

May you shake off any offenses that are still hanging on. May you instead wrap yourself up in the complete love and acceptance of Christ.

May you forgive yourself and forgive others.

May you believe that God's promises are more powerful than your blunders.

May you embrace God's redemptive plan for your life with hope and expectancy.

Be healed and restored as you sleep tonight. And may you wake up with fresh faith and vision for the year ahead.

God bless you!

Special thanks to:

My friends at Bethany House Publishers
You saw the beauty in these blessings

My literary agent, Steve Laube
You gave my message wings

My assistant, Lisa Irwin
You serve in the most excellent way

My intercessors
For your consistent, faithful, powerful prayers

My friends and family
For your presence in my life

My Savior, Jesus
For all that You are to me

SUSIE LARSON is a popular radio host, national speaker, and author. She cohosts the Focus on the Family radio show *Everyday Relationships with Dr. Greg Smalley* and also has her own talk show, *Live the Promise with Susie Larson*. Her passion is to see men and women everywhere strengthened in their faith and mobilized to live out their high calling in Jesus Christ.

Her eight previous books include *Your Beautiful Purpose*, *Growing Grateful Kids*, *The Uncommon Woman*, and *Blessings for the Evening*.

Susie and her husband, Kevin, live near Minneapolis, Minnesota, and have three adult sons, three beautiful daughters-in-law, and one adorable pit bull. For more information, visit www.susielarson.com.

May the Lord bless you
and protect you.

May the Lord smile on you
and be gracious to you.

May the Lord show you his favor
and give you his peace.

NUMBERS 6:24–26 NLT